LOCO

Karen Grossman

DEDICATION

This story is dedicated to my husband, David Grossman, who never stopped encouraging me to write.

Loco

Loco

1
PINK SKY IN THE MORNING

Juan's white pick-up glowed in the Miami-pink sunrise like a mortician's rouge. He puttered around his carport, gathering old bait from his freezer, a bucket, a hand-reel, and an aluminum chair. He heaved all these into the truck bed and slammed the tailgate twice before it latched. After a few cranks, the truck rolled into motion, and Juan headed for the Cuban coffee stand. A Styrofoam cup contained his morning's supply of sugared coffee, which he would consume in shots from a stack of tiny plastic cups.

Juan had bought his truck ten years ago at a government auction, so it bore enough resemblance to an official truck that no one questioned him as he drove past the power company's fence, window down, elbow out, making his way to his secret fishing spot. Some days Juan even gave a friendly wave to power company workers, who would acknowledge him with an unsuspicious nod.

Today Juan encountered no one as he passed through the gate, and drove down a dark mangrove-canopied coral road. When he reached the light at the end of the tunnel of twisted roots, he shut off the truck and sat while it coughed and settled. Then he unloaded the chair, the bucket, the bait and the reel. He took off his white shirt, laid it over the front seat and retrieved the coffee and cups. With everything ready, he sank into his folding chair and took his first shot of coffee. One shot later he put the cups on the upturned bucket and began baiting his line. Easing up from his chair, he extended his hand-held reel slightly over the water. Just as he inhaled to cast his line, he froze. Squinting through sweaty eyelids, his brain held his breath so all faculties could be dedicated to processing a garish image, an arm reaching... a human body, smooth gray and spotted red, clothed, bloated, eyes - no – only one glassy eye staring dead into Juan's.

Juan gasped and choked as some coffee returned to his throat. Backing up he stumbled toward the truck and dropped his reel through the window. He crashed the chair and bucket into the truck bed, grabbed up crumpled bait and coffee cups, fumbled the keys into the ignition and gunned it in reverse, rotating out of the clearing and going a little too fast through the fence, ignoring the approaching power company truck. He was ten minutes away before he realized he was bleeding - a small piece of his skin had caught the hook in his tangled fishing line. He wrapped his finger with the end of his white shirt, slowed to the proper speed, and vanished into the thick morning traffic.

2
RICK AND JOE

Rick O'Donnel was on his third Red Bull, decked out in Florida cracker camper wear, cammo pants, old Guy Harvey T-shirt, faded baseball cap, in a flats boat with his colleague. He and Joe Monroe were veteran undercover agents with the Miami-Dade Police Department. They had stopped calling each other partners when that became increasingly misunderstood for "life partner." Especially because both were divorced half way into their law enforcement career, they wanted everyone to know their relationship was strictly professional. Rick chuckled at the thought of "professional." He and Joe looked anything but, with twin beer guts and messy hair.

After six hours together floating in the everglades, Rick and Joe had run out of things to say. Rick's sunglasses were sliding down the sweat on his nose. As he adjusted his glasses, he saw movement in the distance.

"See that?" he asked Joe. Joe reached for the binoculars.

"No - what?" Joe scanned the horizon.

"Saw some grass moving, and there ain't no breeze," Rick pointed past a dead Florida pine.

Then Joe spotted the motion. "Let's go," he said as he turned the boat. They idled closer to the spot of the movement. At first there appeared to be nothing but a few anhingas drying their wings. Then it surfaced. A ten foot gator. An injured ten foot gator.

"What the . . ." intoned Joe. It looked like a case of animal abuse, the center of the body was compressed and one of his eyes was missing. Something yellow was trailing from its tail. The gator turned belly up, revealing a giant coil of a boa constrictor. Joe put a fish towel over his face.

"Phew..looks like this battle was a draw," Joe snorted through the towel. There was no head on the boa, but a large lump bulged from below where the head should be. "What do you suppose his last meal was - before he tried to eat a gator?" Joe asked. Like a recently shut off water hose, dark liquid trickled from the gator's nostrils and life left it. Rick was already dialing up the game and wildlife officers.

"Guess we'll find out soon enough. Let's call it a day," Rick said.

They rendezvoused with wildlife officers, who took some photos and hauled the animals away for autopsy. Joe and Rick sped off in the opposite direction, to a campsite stocked with satellite wi-fi and phone, fresh water, red bull, junk food and bug spray. Two hours after a peanut butter meal, Rick's phone rang. It was the captain.

"Hey, we need to know exactly where you spotted the gator today," the Captain said.

"Okay, boss, it was in the Everglades, in the water, by an anhinga. I didn't pinpoint a GPS on him. I thought we were looking for a drug deal," Rick replied.

The captain sighed, "The boa was apparently attacked by the gator."

"Oh?" Rick commented. Who cares? He thought.

Thinking he was hiding his sarcastic tone, Rick added, "The boa victim was beheaded by the perpetrator gator. Guess we can close the case!"

"No," the captain continued, "The lump inside the boa was a human arm, shoulder, and part of a torso. The arm bone had rat carcasses stapled to it. This was a fresh kill, Rick. You guys need to get cleaned up and come back in ...tonight. First thing in the morning you'll ride out with uniforms and try to pinpoint your location."

"Stapled rat carcasses? These guys are subtle, huh," said Joe.

As the sun set they loaded fishing gear and supplies, and dismantled the cammo tent, folding it with military precision. Once in the boat they punched in shore coordinates and pulled on night vision goggles. Still, everything looked different at night. The captain's words "fresh kill" were lingering in Rick's mind. Water lapped by the boat, and a breeze was picking up. Suddenly a flood light blinded them.

"Stop and put your hands up!" boomed a male voice.

It was the Miccosukee police. Damn. We didn't even see them with our goggles, thought Rick.

"What are you doing here at night in a boat?" demanded one of the police.

Rick quickly lied, "Sorry, man, we were camping till Joe got a pain in his right side. Tried to call 911 but couldn't get through out here- can you help us?" Joe moaned on cue. Silence from the police boat.

Rick began pleading- "I think a helicopter is his only chance! Please!" Joe's sunburned, sweaty face enhanced his pained expression.

Looking at the others, the officer nodded, "Follow us."

Radios crackled, and soon the rhythmic thunder of a chopper approached.

Joe kept up the act as he was loaded onto the chopper in the middle of Alligator Alley. Rick thanked the Miccosukees as he quickly threw gear in the back of his old Tahoe. He drove off at a respectable speed. By the time he arrived at the hospital, Joe was dressed and coming out of the ER.

"Acute gastritis is the official opinion of the resident. I slipped out when three gunshot victims were brought in," Joe reported.

Rick grinned, "I love the chaos at the public hospital. Did you sign any papers?"

"No, man, I'm unemployed with no insurance - which means I'm *deep* undercover," Joe replied.

"It also means maybe the captain won't find out about the chopper ride."

At daybreak, Joe and Rick showed up at headquarters to catch a ride with the uniforms to the scene.

"Never mind boys," said the captain, "the wildlife guys are going to say they spotted it since it was hauled from your location. We'll examine the area. For now we'll put you on surveillance of a suspected drug condo."

Homicide investigators found only one item of interest sparkling from a blade of everglade grass. It was a necklace commemorating service in the Bay of Pigs invasion. A blade appeared to have been used to scratch out the recipient's name. CSI found traces of blood on the chain that matched the victim's remains.

3
A FREE COUNTRY

Juan awoke on his vinyl chair, the TV still on from last night. He rose from his slouch and stared out the jalousie windows, his mind drifting. The morning news caught his attention.

"Wildlife police made a grisly discovery this morning...." Juan squinted toward the TV.

"A human one-armed torso was pulled from the water. Stay tuned for video of the recovery, which we warn you, is graphic and may disturb some viewers," promised the anchor.

Juan sweated through the commercials. Finally, the news returned and the anchor, with her high-heeled legs crossed under the desk, exclaimed that the arm had been pulled from a python's belly in the everglades. Juan relaxed. He remembered that bodies turning up in odd places happened weekly here. In any event, he assured himself he had no reason to worry. He was not responsible for the dead body. He now was living in a free country.

A free country. Juan had escaped Cuba during the revolution, but he was imprisoned by memories. The doomed efforts of Juan and his compatriots to rid the island of Castro, resulted in nightmares, both waking and sleeping, leaking from the sector of his mind where he stored horrors, suffering, death, the Cuban prison, his wife's accident, and his son's suicide. Lately the seals on the door to this sector had eroded, allowing dark thoughts to emerge and infect his consciousness, and now his favorite fishing spot had been contaminated. Juan sat back down and took a deep, labored breath, wondering how many breaths he had left.

Loneliness and boredom drove Juan to the domino park. He usually avoided the place, because old-timers were full of conspiracy theories about Cuba that invariably left him with a headache and painful memories. But sometimes being alone with his memories was worse.

He was welcomed at the table as if he had never left. After he settled into a folding chair, the questions started.

"Where you been, man? First you disappear, then Raul...." said Adalberto, his sentence trailing as he lit a cigar. Raul had been a friend of Juan's family, and got to know Juan personally during their imprisonment in Cuba. They had lost touch after Raul was released before Juan and had mysteriously wound up in Miami set up in a nice house. Raul was a vocal opponent of the Castro regime, and everyone suspected a prominent member of the exile community rewarded him. Juan had been vocal about his opposition for years. But age, sickness, and family tragedy made him more of a broken opponent. He did not have the mental energy to carry on about politics. He had just enough energy to carry on.

"*Ay*, my health, my health, but I feel better now," replied Juan. He played as in a trance, surprised at how he enjoyed the company. Then the subject returned to Raul. He had been coming regularly, and just did not show up several days ago. Someone said he ran off with his barber Berti- a girl who flirted with all the old men on *Calle Ocho*. She had disappeared about the same time. But no one knew. The house in Westchester had a for sale sign and looked abandoned.

"I bet you Castro had him offed," said Marco, who made a throat slitting motion with his cigar. Everyone shook their heads in agreement. No one would put it past Castro.

When Juan drove home from the park, he felt comfortable. The cigar smoke had not brought out his cough. He had even managed to laugh a few times. It felt good. He would go back tomorrow.

4

INTRUDERS

The next morning Juan arrived at the park with coffee for everyone. As soon as he approached the table he felt a wave of tension.

"Que paso?" he asked.

"You just missed Yoli." –the sister of Berti - " replied Manny.

"Oh – Berti the barber?" Juan asked.

"Si. She's crazy desperate looking for Berti - she thinks Raul was involved in something . . . heavy," Manny said as he arranged the dominoes.

"Like what, drugs?" Juan asked putting down the coffee.

"She never saw no drugs and swears Berti would not be around no one like that," Manny explained.

Here we go thought Juan. Here come the conspiracy theories.

"Raul was in the brigade, no?" said Manny slowly.

Juan pulled out a cigar. It was going to be a bad morning. He played for an hour, tuning out the conspiracy theorists. At noon he devised an exit strategy.

"*Ay dios mio* I forgot my daughter is bringing me lunch ... *'ta luego*."

Juan left the guys to their reminiscing and drove back to his small house. He entered just in time to see the TV weather girl being interrupted.

"News Alert!" The TV blared. "Another grim discovery today. Police are reporting that a dead body has been discovered on government property - kayakers noticed a human arm among the mangroves." Juan sat down hard, locking his arms to the edges of his chair.

A young tanned girl in the arm of her boyfriend, eyes shining explained. "I thought I saw some trash, some white thing I thought we should pick up and throw away."

Her boyfriend interrupted, "this dead gray arm was holding up a plastic Cuban coffee cup - I guess he needed some energy - it was creepy."

Switch to live coverage of gloved detectives combing the area. Then an FPL spokesman indicating the area was unused by the company, but was sometimes used by kayakers and fisherman, though it was clearly marked "No Trespassing."

"We'll be reviewing our surveillance film to determine whether any intruders can be identified," the power company spokesman said with a determined grimace.

Intruder - Juan's heart began pounding.

A knock at the door jolted Juan. He guiltily shut off the TV to listen. "Intruder" reverberated in his mind.

"Papi? Are you there?" asked his daughter, Mirta.

Juan took his time getting to the door. "I forgot you were coming over."

"Are you okay? Have you taken your blood pressure today? You're sweating and it's 100 degrees in here!" Mirta yelled.

He let Mirta lead him back to the couch. "I'll get you some water. I wasn't going to come over but I'm glad I did - when is your next doctor's appointment?" she asked.

"Next week," said Juan without thinking.

"Good. I brought you some leftover rice. I came over earlier and you weren't here - were you fishing?" Mirta asked.

"No - I went to the park to play dominoes," Juan mumbled.

"Oh that explains it. Those friends of yours just bring up bad memories. I don't think you should go anymore," Mirta said as she handed him a plate.

"I'm fine. I go back pretty far with those guys," said Juan as he took his first mouthful.

"I know Papi. I just worry about you," Mirta said, inhaling deeply.

"No te preocupe. Esta bien." Juan said as he forced a smile. "You just came for the rice?"

"Oh, no, I almost forgot that a package came to our house addressed to you - there's no return address. Were you expecting something?" Mirta asked.

Juan quickly lied "*si...* c-pap machine attachment - they must have your address from when I came home from the hospital. Thank you for bringing it." He smiled again.

Mirta's phone played a loud two-second Marc Anthony salsa.

"Okay, I gotta go Papi." Mirta said with a kiss and then she was gone.

Juan watched her pull away and went back to the chair. First things first. They found the body he found. It had to be the same body. He remembered the outstretched fingers, the one eye, then a blur. I just got out of there. I had coffee, but I took it with me. He remembered the stack of small cups. One could have blown to the corpse's fingertips. Or possibly it was someone else's trash. "Could it be traced to me?" wondered Juan. Seemed unlikely. Then the newscast "intruders." "I've never seen any cameras around there. Worst case scenario is they question me. I didn't do anything wrong! Except 'intrude' on government property to fish," Juan assured himself.

Now, the package. After holding it a minute he considered the possibility of a bomb. "I'm crazy. I do spend too much time with the domino boys," thought Juan as he went to the kitchen. Still his hand shook as he got a paring knife and carefully slid open the brown paper. In it was an old cigar box. Cuban cigars. He put it on the kitchen counter. Vaguely hopeful, he opened the lid. Staring up at him was a photo of Raul. Beneath the photo was Raul's wallet. Beneath Raul's wallet was Raul's passport. Beneath Raul's passport was a Ziploc bag with a brown piece of meat - it looked like a piece of liver but with a coarser texture. Recognition came with a heaving reflex - it was a human tongue - Raul's tongue. Juan's fingers could no longer hold the box. He blacked out.

Loco

5

EYES OPEN; MOUTH SHUT

It was pitch black when Juan came to. He lay on the cool terrazzo floor; slowly becoming aware of where he was and reconstructing what led him to this spot. The phone was ringing. He grabbed the receiver. The caller clicked off. Juan turned on a small light and closed all the blinds. He sat on the kitchen floor and eyed the cigar box on the counter.

The message was clear. Raul talked. He was brutally murdered. If you talk, the same will happen to you. But Juan could not think of any information he had. What did someone think he knew?

Whoever sent the package thought he was still living at his daughter's house. He had left a month ago. After his last hospitalization, he recovered there. It started off well. Mirta cooked for him and talked. Then there was Sophie and Carlos, his grandchildren. They gave him hope. Mirta's husband drove trucks. He tolerated Juan when he was home. Rising gas prices gradually increased Mirta's husband's home time. Eventually Juan thought moving back to his home would be better for everyone.

On the floor with his back against the cabinets, Juan recalled it was the same position he had used sitting in prison until the jailers concluded he was mentally impaired and not worth keeping. He credited his own survival to the credo passed down by his father: "Keep your eyes open and your mouth shut." He had no intention of talking to anyone about anything.

On the other hand, he had to make a decision about what to do with the cigar box. He thought of how he could assure those responsible he would not say anything about anything. But he had no idea with whom Raul was involved or what he supposedly knew. He would have to become a regular at the dominos park and keep his ears open. In the meantime, he would wrap the box in plastic and put it under his bait in the freezer. His daughter would never come across it there.

6
AHCHOKO

Ahchoko inhaled the morning air, a thick mix of humidity and greasy smoke from the morning's bread. His eyes followed his grandsons, officers in the Miccosukee police force. They were just getting home from a meeting with Miami-Dade police over the body found in the gator/boa tangle. They came to report to him, as they always did.

Ahchoko had sent them out to watch the undercover drug agents camped in the swamp. He knew the agents had been staking out the area for weeks, but the Chief had not seen anything unusual until the night of the festival to kick off Miccosukee Days, a tourist event the gamers organized. Amidst the crowd that evening he saw some men he surmised were *nonchois* - up to no good. Perhaps they were the drug dealers the undercovers were looking for. But something wasn't right. These guys were not flashy, and they wore long sleeves despite the heat. Their hair was dark and slicked against their head. They were small, not the muscle for a gang, that's for sure. Ahchoko always associated people with certain animals. These guys looked like black otters. Small dark eyes, slippery characters.

His grandsons relayed the information from the police. Ahchoko nodded and retreated to his bed. He felt uneasy about a crime having been committed under his nose. There was only one explanation for how it could have happened. Outsiders must have discovered the tunnels.

7
WHALE

Popping open an ice cold Diet Coke, Joe chortled, "they PAY us for doing this." Rick leaned back in the 23' Mako open fisherman boat.

"We're surveilling the area for suspicious activity. Don't forget to turn on the fish finder. The water is not that clear today, and it's flat as a board." Rick replied.

They were actually watching a Brickell condo with military grade scopes and cameras mounted on the center console as they drifted in Biscayne Bay. An inordinate amount of electricity was being utilized in the unit, and a tipster suspected a grow house operation. The best view into the unit just happened to be from the bay.

"Let's catch some grunts for lunch," Rick suggested as he baited the hook with some squid. Joe kept his eyes on the fish finder.

Rick noticed and yelled, "no grunt's gonna show up on the fish finder." As Joe backed away from the display, something dark caught his eye. A huge shadow passed right beneath them.

"Holy crap! What's that?" Joe yelled as the boat rose in a rogue swell. The shadow was gone. "We're in 30 feet of water. I think a whale passed under us." Joe offered.

"A whale? You idiot. Whales don't live in Biscayne Bay." Rick retorted.

"Maybe it's lost, like those pilot whales in the key," Joe reasoned.

"I don't think pilot whales are 20 feet long, and besides....

Rick was interrupted by the concussion of an explosion that rocked the boat.

"It's the condo!" Shards of glass and debris blew out from the balcony of the very unit they were watching.

Rick radioed, "All units fire and explosion at Brickell Bay 17th floor, all units."

Then he phoned the captain. "Hey the unit just exploded. I think we have it on film. We just set up. I'll have to check the cameras. . . .Okay, we're getting out of sight."

They sped back to a private dock south of Coral Gables. They were to clean up and be downtown at 3:00 p.m. for a de-briefing. They came in under the building, parked in the garage and took the dedicated elevator to the undercover detective department. The captain was waiting for them.

"Let's see what you got," the captain said as he approached.

Joe uploaded the raw film to the display, which unfortunately still had the sound on it. At first the captain shook his head, "You guys get film of the actual unit exploding, and you sound like a bunch of morons!"

The captain grew silent, thinking. Joe and Rick looked down, each speculating about the punishment the captain might be considering.

Finally, the Captain spoke, "What's this about a whale."

"We're sorry about the talk, boss, we were just setting up and then we were going to be all business," Rick explained.

"No, does the fish finder have a printout?" Captain asked.

"Seriously? You want to see a picture of the whale?" Joe asked.

"No," the Captain said with a serious face, . . . "I want to see a picture of a drug sub."

8
KEEP IN TOUCH

The DEA was well aware of modified subs used by drug dealers off the coast of South America. But the shallow waters of Biscayne Bay seemed an especially risky place to operate, and frankly there were so many easier ways to get drugs into Miami, it seemed an odd choice of methods. So with much skepticism DEA agent Carly Bloom came for a consult with Miami undercover. Carly wore black pants, rubber-soled pumps and a light oversized jacket. This work outfit best concealed her weapons and her figure, both of which she was hyperconscious in the presence of the male-dominated Miami-Dade Police Department.

The captain made the introductions. "Agent Bloom, these are my detectives, Joe Monroe and Rick O'Donnel. They were on the boat at the time of the explosion."

She nodded, "Detectives, first I'd like to see the film, then the printout, and then I'll have some questions."

She stifled a grin at the dialogue about grunts and whales. The film angle changed before the explosion, presumably at the point of the unusual swell.

"Okay, pass me the printout," she said. If it hadn't been for the printout she wouldn't even be there, so unlikely was the idea of a local drug sub.

"You're right captain, it's not a fish. It looks like a drug sub, but it could be an amateur sub user or a marine scientist. I'm going to consult with a sub expert. As far as the explosion, we've found that it was remotely triggered via cell phone, which pretty much eliminates the chance it was detonated from a sub. If it was a drug sub, keep in mind it could go all the way up the Miami River. Keep your ears to the ground about any deliveries along that route of something super high end. I don't think they would take such a risk with a small load," Carly said. She had no questions yet.

Carly gathered her papers and rose, extending her hand. "Nice to have met you, keep in touch."

After the door shut behind her, Joe said, "Captain, she wants you to keep in *touch*."

"Shut up you. I'm sending you guys back to the Everglades to lie low for a while. Take enough peanut butter for a week, but not enough to make you sick. I would hate for you to have *acute gastritis* Joe," sneered the captain as he gestured artificial quotes in the air.

"Thanks for your concern Captain," Joe sheepishly replied.

"Just stick around here for a few hours in case the DEA needs something else," said the Captain as he shut the door to his office.

9
FUGITIVE

Juan returned to the domino park. The usual welcome comforted him. He reminded himself to listen carefully, not to let his mind drift.

"*Oye – chica loca*" Adalberto mumbled.

Juan looked up. Yoli approached the table, looking pale and desperate. She opened her mouth to speak, but then collapsed in sobs. All the men got up to offer her a seat. Chokingly the words came out.

"Police.... found...Raul," she stared at the table.

The men were wholly focused on Yoli and she continued, "He was murdered." Groans swelled from the old men. "He was found in the Everglades, just his arm, his torso, and his Bay of Pigs necklace. They won't tell me anything else! Nothing about Berti. The police questioned me for two hours, but I don't know anything! They want to talk to all of Raul's friends."

A police cruiser appeared on cue. Shock silenced the table as the uniforms approached.

"You gentlemen have heard the news about Raul. We'd like you all to come down to the station to help us find the guys who did this," said a serious officer.

Adalberto was the first to respond. "Of course."

The interviews lasted several hours. Juan and the other old men exited the station wearing faces red with stress, increased blood pressure and severe nicotine fit.

"What did you get?" asked the Captain.

"Oh, we solved the case, they all agree on the same suspect," said Officer Manny Wright.

"Really-great!" said the Captain.

"Yeah, um they all think it was Castro," explained Wright.

"As in Fidel Castro?" asked the Captain.

"Yeah, these interviews were like a conspiracy theory marathon. Useless."

Joe fingered the dull pencils abandoned in his dusty desk drawer. Offices made him antsy. Because of the suspected drug connection and the fact that they inadvertently discovered the body, Joe and Rick had watched the interviews through closed circuit TV.

"Hey Captain- You gotta warrant to go get Castro? We gotta boat," joked undercover Joe. "Seriously, the one guy looked super nervous – Juan somebody?"

"They were all spooked. Juan has been in Cuban prison, just like Raul. Served in the Brigade. I don't think he feels too comfortable at police headquarters," said the captain.

"Maybe we should visit him at his house, where he might be more comfortable," suggested Joe. "It's on the way to the trail – we could just do a drive-by, and then continue to our spot."

"OK," said the Captain. "Let's wait for his interview to get typed up and then tell him he needs to sign it."

Joe and Rick surveyed the office to see whether anyone had brought food into the kitchen. Stale bagel parts were scattered on a plastic plate. The coffee pot had a half-inch of tar-black liquid on the bottom.

"I think I'll wait for the quick mart," said Rick.

Thirty minutes later the Captain emerged from his office with a lab report in his hand. "Hey you heard about the dead John Doe in the FPL mangroves? Guess whose DNA was on him… Juan Espinosa."

"The nervous domino player? Are you kidding?" asked Joe.

"Well actually it was taken from the Cuban coffee cup the stiff was holding. We need to ramp up on this guy, but first let's get a search warrant for his property. I don't believe in coincidences. If this guy knew Raul and had coffee with John Doe he knows something major he isn't telling us. Let's watch him while the warrant is getting processed. Perfect assignment for you and Rick, even if you're not in a boat," said the captain.

The weekend of surveillance showed Juan stayed home with one visitor, his daughter with a bag of food. Monday morning he went out and was followed to the domino park.

"Anybody else at this table being watched?" Juan asked. The group was surprised because Juan usually avoided their paranoid conversations. Juan described the white van with gringos posing as plumbers. "I am not going back to prison no matter what-what do they want from me?"

"Maybe you better disappear for a while – Yoli has a duplex she used to share with her sister." Adalberto used his phone. "Yoli says to go to the barber and she'll meet you at the back door."

Juan waited for a moving truck to block the van's view and slipped onto a bus going in the direction of the barber.

"Hey Juan left the park and I lost him," Joe complained to Rick.

Rick answered, "the other guys there? Get a uniform to ask them where he went."

When asked, the group said they thought he left to go home or maybe a haircut. Joe and Rick returned to Juan's house, at the same moment the search warrant was being executed.

"Got a lot of nothing here. Old man clothes, TV, coffee cups, photos," said a detective.

"Take the photos," Rick said.

"All done inside? On to the carport," said Rick as he and Joe did a quick glance around.

"Looks like a broken washer, no clothes inside, an old freezer – hey maybe the rest of the dead guy's in here." Joe said as he reached in. He groped around a haphazard stack of frozen chunks of bait.

"Looks like bait, bait, um….get CSI here, there's a Cuban cigar box in plastic," Rick said as he made room for the CSI detectives and photographers.

Gloved special officers brought the box into the kitchen and spread its contents on the table: Raul's personal items, and the frozen tongue.

"What a nut – he kept the guy's tongue in the freezer! Disgusting," Joe said as he coughed and turned away.

"It's all yours," Rick said, handing the envelope with Juan's statement to the homicide detectives.

"Let's get out to the glades before I start to feel like a real detective," said Joe as they passed under the crime tape being strung around the carport.

10
DOCHI

Rick and Joe stopped by the quick mart just before the Trail to load up on Red Bull.

"Feeling better?" asked the clerk. Dochi Billie was the youngest granddaughter of Chief Ahchoko.

"Uh, yeah, thanks," said Joe slowly.

"News travels like a brush fire around here," she added by way of explanation. Then she handed them a gear bag. "This was by your boat when you left in such a hurry."

"Oh," said Rick, slightly embarrassed. "Must have our night fishing glasses in there."

"Yeah, ...night fishing..." the clerk intoned.

Joe took the bag and they got in the truck.

"She totally made us, Rick," groaned Joe.

"Her and everyone else out here probably," said Rick.

As they made their way down Tamiami Trail, lights flashed behind the truck. Miccosukee police. Rick reluctantly pulled over.

Officer Billie approached the truck. "Hello gentlemen. License and registration."

As Joe rooted in the glove compartment, Billie leaned closer to Rick.

"We know who you are and what you're doing here. Next time you need to get out of here just ask for a ride, not a damn helicopter evacuation," said Billie in a disgusted tone.

"How'd you sneak up on us out there?" Rick ventured.

Billie lowered his voice "Ancient Trail people secret." He waved off the registration. "All you need to know is, if you actually hear people coming at night, it ain't us."

11

INVESTIGATION

Mirta debated answering the phone when the caller ID showed her father's neighbor, Mari, was calling. I'm sure she needs something and I'm not planning on going over there today, thought Mirta. After the third ring, however, concern for her father drove her to pick up the phone.

"Mirta!, are you ok?" Mari blurted.

"*Si,*" Mirta started.

"What happened to your father? There are police cars everywhere, blocking our whole street!" Mari was still talking.

Mirta dropped the receiver and ran out to the car. An instant later she pulled over and ran to her father's house, tears in her eyes. After she explained who she was, an officer escorted her to the house.

"Where is your father?" he asked in a sober tone.

"I don't understand – is he okay? What are you doing here?" Mirta started shaking.

An older officer led her to the living room couch. "Sit down and let's talk a minute. When was the last time you saw your father?" Mirta couldn't think clearly with the commotion around her father's home. Voices seemed to echo from the terrazzo floors to the plastered walls. Humidity was fogging up the jalousie windows and she felt dizzy. "Y-y-yesterday after mass we came by and brought him lunch," Mirta managed to say.

"We think it would be a good idea if you come down to the station to try to help us find him. We are concerned that he has gone missing." The officer's voice sounded more angry than concerned. Nothing made sense as Mirta entered the police cruiser, and every neighbor eyed their slow drive away.

The police station interrogation centered on identifying everyone her father knew, for how long he knew them, whether he was involved in drugs, and his history with the Bay of Pigs invasion. Mirta never paid attention to the talk that had so long upset her father and mother. She focused on her brother, a Navy hero. She described her father as an old man in poor health. He had been hospitalized not long ago. She was worried about him moving back alone and not taking care of himself. He had even stopped fishing….there were questions about his fishing, exactly *where* did he fish. "It was a *secret* spot!" Mirta said with her hands shaking.

Why did he keep it a secret? The police wanted to know. Finally she was so in tears and exhausted they let her leave. Her husband emerged from another interview with an angry look on his face.

"*Vamos*" was all he said as they went to his truck.

12

YOLI

Yoli made Juan a real Cuban coffee and a home-cooked meal.

"Thank you, Yoli," Juan said as he cleaned his plate. She showed him to a bedroom and Juan fell into an exhausted sleep as soon as he felt the pillow.

As black turned to gray, Juan awoke, shuffled to the kitchen and splashed water on his face. Yoli sat up from the couch.

"Juan – do you feel better? Can we talk?" she asked.

"*Si* Yoli," Juan said gratefully.

Yoli made a breakfast of coffee and Cuban toast. "Chanel 7 says you are a missing murder suspect – a suspect in the murder of *Raul*." She took a long drag off her cigarette as that sunk in to Juan's brain.

"Yoli," Juan began in a deliberate tone, "I know Raul was murdered, but I don't know who did it or why they did it. I swear on the grave of my wife and son. You have to believe me."

"Of course I believe you or you wouldn't be here," Yoli said. Juan slowly processed that he was now a fugitive in a murder investigation. Juan's hands were starting to tremble.

"Here have a cigarette Papi." Yoli offered.

On his third try Juan lit the cigarette. Yoli continued, "A friend of mine who works at Miami-Dade says the police think you're involved in TWO murders. Sounds like you really need to disappear. I just want to know what you know about Raul and Berti. I know they weren't involved in drugs. According to Berti, Raul said crazy things about Castro. She said Raul heard Castro was dying of cancer and vowed revenge on the Miami exiles as his last wish."

Rolling his eyes, Jaun softly spoke, "Yoli, I know Castro has spies in Miami, but do you really think he would go after a bunch of old men for something that failed fifty years ago? Castro may be evil, even the devil, but he hasn't killed us after all these years. Why would he even try at this point?"

"I'm just telling you what Berti said. Who knows, maybe Castro has finally lost his mind completely. Why do the police even suspect you?" asked Yoli.

Juan told Yoli everything, including the body at the Bay and the cigar box. He assured her there was nothing in the box to show that Berti had been murdered.

"Who was the body at the bay?" asked Yoli.

"I don't know – I didn't recognize – he couldn't be recognized" Juan's hands were rubbing his head. "I need some air."

"Write down the medicine you take and I'll get the pharmacist in Hialeah to get it for me. Do you trust the guys at the park?" asked Yoli.

"Yes like brothers," nodded Juan.

"I'm going to visit them and tell them you are innocent. I'm going to ask them if they know anything about Berti, then I'm going to the barber to look through her stuff again. I'll be back after dark for dinner."

"Make sure you aren't followed," cautioned Juan.

He went back to the bedroom and turned on the ceiling fan. His head was spinning as he got into bed. The rotating fan pushed thick air onto Juan, sending him down a familiar tunnel of paranoia.

13

THE NOTEBOOK

Yoli got Juan's medicine from a pharmacist who still dispensed drugs without a prescription, and headed to the barbershop where Berti worked.

"Anything new?" asked Yoli as she walked inside.

"The police think Juan killed him. Now Juan is on the run," said Jose, busily tending to a man with practically no hair.

Looking at an empty station, Yoli coughed as she felt tears welling up, "I just want Berti back."

Momentarily stopping the clipping motions, Jose softened, "I put her things in a bag for you, things the police didn't want. Take them if that will make you feel better."

"Thank you Jose," Yoli gave Jose a kiss, retrieved the bag, and left. Her next planned stop was the park, but the men were in a huddle with a Miami-Dade cop. Yoli gunned her civic past them and drove west on 8th street.

With no clear plan she turned on talk radio. "Another disappearance and possible murder rocks the exile community. Armando Francisco Ortega, Bay of Pigs veteran and beloved member of our community has disappeared," the reporter announced. "Is it murder, or just a coincidence among old men? What are the police doing to try to solve this?" Yoli started driving to the duplex.

Juan was loudly snoring when she put Berti's bag on the table. Yoli was grateful for the privacy while she tearfully sorted through Berti's things. Of course the police wouldn't want this stuff. A plastic rose in a plastic vase. A plastic rosary. Treasure to Berti, trash to the police. Yoli fingered the beads on the rosary. "Oh Berti, where are you?" she silently pleaded with a heavy sigh. The only things of value were Berti's scissors, in a leather-zippered case. Yoli absently unrolled the case flat on the table. Only it wasn't flat. A rectangular bulge stretched the elastic holding in one of the scissors. Yoli carefully lifted the seam of the case, and pulled out a notebook. Probably her client list, thought Yoli. She opened the cover to reveal a list of names not in Berti's handwriting. Then she began nervously reading.

14

SUBS

With nothing going on in the glades, Rick and Joe returned to headquarters to file their weekly report of nothing.

Things at police headquarters were hotter than usual, unsolved disappearances, unsolved murders and two disgruntled undercover officers in a conference room.

"I hate meetings," complained Joe.

"Really? I never knew that about you." intoned Rick.

The captain barged in, "Know what was in the drug condo? Nothing. No drugs. Just explosives. Russian military explosives. Someone seems to have blown it up for no reason. No reason except it coincided with a certain submarine making its way to the Miami River. Did your informants tell you anything whatsoever about any drug deliveries along the Miami River?? No??" You have any idea how far up the Miami River goes?? Follow that river to the freaking reservation and don't resurface around here until you have something useful." Door slams.

"Dang haven't seen captain that worked up in a while," observed Rick.

The body from the mangroves had now been identified. At first thought to be a former Brigade member, he was the nephew of a Brigade member who shared the same name. The homicide detectives were trying to find a connection between Juan and the victim.

"Well, you don't have to ask me twice to go back to our camp. Let's go," Joe said, heading towards the elevator.

15

SPIES LIKE US

Juan woke up to the smell of *sofrito* on the stove. Yoli looked strangely peaceful, almost in a trance as she stirred the garlic and onion sauté. She silently brought Juan some bread and coffee. She turned the stove to simmer and sat down with Juan.

"Armando Ortega is missing. I know you didn't have anything to do with it because you were here with me. I think I know what is going on, but you are not going to believe it," Yoli said as she turned to Juan.

She put the small notebook on the table. "This was in Berti's scissor case. It is Raul's journal. Juan, Raul was working for the CIA. He pretended to work for Castro's spies, but he was working for the CIA. Raul kept this journal of what he found out. Juan, according to this journal, Castro is planning an all-out attack on Miami, first on the exiles he thinks are the prime betrayers (those survivors of the Bay of Pigs invasion) and then ending with an underground explosion to blow up downtown and specific elite Cuban exile areas." She pushed the notebook over to Juan. "Open it! Read it!"

Juan took Yoli's hands in his. "Yoli, listen to me. Castro is an old man. We are old too. When you get old and people die or disappear, you want to think it is his fault. Maybe Berti and Raul believed this, but I don't."

Yoli's face reddened. "You won't even read this? You don't want to know what will happen? You can't put your head in the sand every time something is too painful to bear. At some point, you have to face it and deal with it. Like Santiago!"

Juan froze. "You bring up my son with this? My son was a hero, a Navy seal!"

"Yes he was Juan. But I don't believe his death was a suicide. Neither did your wife. But you wouldn't pursue it because you didn't want to get involved in another conspiracy. You didn't want people to call you a crazy old man, even if it meant finding out the truth about your son's death. You didn't want to question your wife's accident; you didn't want to face the possibility that you couldn't protect them from Castro's spies! Yes you are an old man, Castro is an old man too. Are you going to let that old man hurt your daughter and grandchildren as well? Are you going to go to your grave knowing you were too much of a coward to save them? What are you living for anyway?"

Yoli's words stopped when the expression on Juan's face – the pain turned to anguish – showed her she had gone too far. Juan took Raul's journal and stumbled into the bedroom, slamming the door. Rattled, Yoli took a cigarette out and lit it.

16

THE RESERVATION

Joe and Rick breezed into the quick mart. Joe looked around for Dochi. A large silent Miccosukee clerk rang them up. As they were finishing packing ice in a cooler outside, Joe turned around to see the clerk behind him. Joe said, "Hey, what's up.....Dochi not working today?"

"Ahchoko wants to talk to you, come this way." The expressionless clerk said. Joe and Rick exchanged glances.

"Okay, sure," they said. Joe and Rick both thought the old Miccosukee chief would lecture them about life in the glades, the helicopter, their boundaries, etc. The clerk led them to an airboat behind the store. Both Rick and Joe were conscious of their ankle strapped firearms as they tried to casually step onto the boat. There is never talking on an airboat when the blades are roaring, and this ride seemed unusually long, so that the two were sure they would be well out of Wi-Fi range, wherever they were headed.

At last they reached the encampment. People milled about huts with lowered eyes stealing suspicious glances at Joe and Rick. Even the mosquitoes seemed wary. The clerk led them through a blanketed door and left them alone with Chief Ahchoko. He motioned them to sit down.

One of Chief's grandson's entered the hut. "We have a problem. One of our people surprised a strange man on our land. He tried to hurt her. As she screamed, her brother heard her and tried to fight the man. But the man got away and then was attacked by a python. We would like you to remove the body."

"That's it? That's the story?" Joe asked.

"This man was trespassing, violating our land with some metal container. We would like you to remove it as well," added the grandson.

"Show us the body and the container." Rick sputtered. Chief Ahchoko said nothing, but his eyes danced.

"May we talk to the person he attacked?" asked Joe.

"No we have done our own investigation," said the grandson, lifting the blanket and ushering them out.

Behind the reservation lay a submarine, cut in thirds, and a bloated figure of a man lay next to the sub. "Where's the python?" Joe asked.

"It has been disposed of." The chief's grandson replied.

"Look, this is a submarine! It goes under water. Where did you find this?" yelled Joe.

"I don't know what he was doing with it but you may remove it." With that the chief's grandson motioned some men to hook up a trailer to the airboat and they began loading sections of the submarine on the trailer. Women brought some blankets and plastic and rolled the body inside of it. The young men added it to the load and draped plastic over the entire load. Joe unsuccessfully tried his cell phone. The satellite phone was locked in the Tahoe. There was no choice but to ride back with the load and phone the captain once they got a signal.

When they arrived near the quick mart Rick got the captain on the phone. "Go to your campsite and set up. I don't want your location connected with this at all. I'm sending out units to recover the body and the debris. Call in tonight for a briefing," the captain instructed.

Rick and Joe waited for the police lights to appear on the horizon and pulled away to their launching site. They found their camp area as they had left it.

"You know the girl had to be Dochi," Joe said.

"No I don't know that, maybe today was her day off," Rick answered.

"How does a submarine get to the reservation? The water is no way deep enough. How did that guy die? I think it was a person, not a python. Or they knocked him out and put him in with a python," Joe speculated.

"The ME will tell us how he died and hopefully who he is. The guy was probably a drug dealer trying to dispose of the submarine," Rick said.

The captain had no information on the sub or the identity of the corpse that night. Joe and Rick fell into a fitful sleep.

17

CULTURE SHOCK

The next morning after a patrol around the glades, Joe called in and spoke to the Captain's assistant, Shawna.

"You heard?" she started.

"No we're in the glades – heard what?" Joe asked.

"All hell has broken loose. Valladeros restaurant exploded and burned to the ground last night. People died. You guys are lucky to be out there. People are protesting that the police have ignored the exile community. They claim they are under attack." Shawna relayed breathlessly. "Captain is trying to calm everything down but we just found out . . . (dramatic pause) …the mayor is missing," Shawna whispered.

18

THE CALLING

Yoli turned from the stove at the sound of Juan emerging from the bedroom. He looked revitalized. "I read the journal." He came over to the table and took the plastic rosary in his hand. "I swear by the Virgin Mary, so help me God I will use my last breath to fight the dictator and save our children and grandchildren. And, God willing, I will go back to Cuba with my brothers and finish what we started."

Yoli was surprised and a little concerned about Juan. That look in his eyes did not seem quite rational, yet Yoli hugged him tightly. She would visit the park and enlist the help of Juan's friends.

19

SANCTUARY

The rectory at St. Mary's had an air of privacy. It contained one of the few basements in a Miami structure. In it were stored rarely seen relics as well as documents of the Pedro Pan evacuation of Cuban children carried out by the church in the 1950's. This was where Juan and his compatriots held their meeting.

"Gentlemen," started Juan, "Raul was murdered by Castro's agents here in Miami after they discovered he was working for the CIA. When he was murdered he was about to share Castro's attack plan with the public, because the CIA did not take him seriously. I have here his journal with details of Castro's plan. You know Raul's girlfriend Berti is still missing, as well as Armando. Now our mayor is also missing, and the explosion killed twelve Cuban-Americans. Raul predicted everything that is happening in his journal. The police believe I am responsible for murder. When we were interviewed about Raul the police believed we were a bunch of crazy paranoid old men. The fact is Castro is attacking us here today. I come to you tonight as an old man. Many of you are old men too. But we are not too old to make a difference. We are alive for a reason. That reason is to finish what we started years ago. This time, my friends, we are going to destroy Castro OUR way. We have the intelligence, we have the community, and we have the Lord to protect us," Juan's voice boomed in the cavernous basement. People straightened in their chairs. No one doubted the facts.

"Raul's journal tells exactly how Castro intends to destroy the exile community. There are secret underground passage ways extending from the mouth of the Miami River, under downtown and all the way to the Everglades," Juan explained.

Father Pedro rolled a chalkboard behind Juan. Juan began diagramming the underground tunnels depicted in the journal. Lists of weapons were recorded. Those with small boats were enlisted to investigate possible tunnel sites and to participate in the defense. The use of small planes was discussed. The next meeting was scheduled, and Juan was energized.

20
UNDERGROUND

Mirta shook the priest's hand on her way out of daily mass. He pressed something into her hand. A note of support he said, read it when you get home. Mirta unfolded the note alone in her kitchen. "Dearest Mirta, I am well. I am on a mission to save you and your family. Please kiss the children. Know that I love you, Papi." She held the note to her heart and wept.

Joe and Rick drove the boat to the quick mart to restock. Dochi was behind the counter. Joe was visibly relieved to see her.

"Hey! Good to see you, what's happening?" Joe said with a smile.

"You tell me," she said hesitantly. Joe and Rick looked at each other and shrugged.

"You really don't know,........." she said. Tears came to her eyes and Joe put his hand on her shoulder.

"Come outside, away from the store cameras," she said.

Once outside Joe said, "Hey look, I thought it was you who was hurt."

"No, I'm fine," Dochi said. "My brother got the guy before he hurt me, he just surprised me. I'm really scared of what is going on here underground. What can you tell me to help us?"

Joe misunderstood, "Well you never know what's going on behind the scenes, but I will help you if I can."

"No, I mean really underground, under the river, under the earth. You don't know about the tunnels do you?" Dochi asked. Joe and Rick looked at each other. "Follow me," Dochi said, walking towards a canal.

She led them to the back of the mart and through a path of tall grass. They came upon an opening the size of a person. "This way," she said as she disappeared into the dark. Joe and Rick followed and quickly could stand in a limestone cave.

"This is pretty cool!" Rick said.

"The ancient trail people used these caves and tunnels to navigate the river to the ocean, and for battle. Some of our ancestors are buried here. It was a secret for generations; it is sacred to us. Then we discovered others were using them. Let me show you what we've found." Dochi led Joe and Rick through a long tunnel that opened to a lagoon with a small boat.

"Get in," Dochi said, sitting down at the motor. Joe, Rick and Dochi spent the rest of the day weaving through tunnels and open water, stopping at caves and finding rockets, guns and explosives. The mouth of the Miami River contained the largest of the caves, somewhere beneath an ancient ceremonial site now dubbed "the Miami Circle." There, Dochi's brother was waiting for them.

"What do you think of all this?" he asked.

"We've got to report it to our captain asap!" Joe's voice echoed in the cavern. Several Miccosukees emerged from the darkness in front of and behind Joe and Rick.

"No you don't," said an old man as he put a cloth over Joe's mouth. Joe's last memory was the swishing of a white pony tail, and the thud of Rick's shoulder against his.

21

MULTI-AGENCY BRIEFING

DEA Agent Carly Bloom was back in town to inspect the drug sub. Her FBI colleague Agent Woodward accompanied her to the hangar where the debris from the sub was stored. "No drugs" she concluded after walking through the sheared steel.

"Agreed" said Woodward. "This looks like another payload, like weapons, maybe weapons for drug dealers?" Woodward posited.

"Doesn't make sense." Bloom mused. "Let's go back to headquarters and see what the agents are finding out about the explosions, I heard they think it might be related to some underground exile terrorist group."

"There are no such groups on our radar – we'll check with CIA- whatever is going on I don't know who has the weapons but we better find out soon." Woodward cautioned.

They arrived just as a multi-agency briefing was beginning. CIA operative supervisor Hammond was speaking. "Raul was on our payroll, deep undercover, investigating activities of Cuban agents in Miami. He had told his contact there was some sort of invasion being organized against exiles in Miami. It was supposedly Castro's dying wish that he blow up the city – with prominent exiles as specific targets. He was to start with Bay of Pigs survivors, and .."

"Sorry to interrupt, but what credibility do you give to Raul's claims here, I mean wasn't he a survivor and probably paranoid? Do you have anything other than this old guy's word to back up his theory? This doesn't really pass our straight face test around here, with all due respect" Captain challenged Hammond.

Woodward added, "FBI has found no evidence of organized activity against the exile community as a whole. We have heard no chatter about explosions or bombs coming from Cuba." Nods in agreement moved like a wave across the room.

"Excuse me," said a female in the back of the room.

"Shawna?" said the Captain. "Please Captain, I have lived here my whole life. You came down from Boston, what three years ago? Please hear me out. No computer trail? No chatter? When I go to the Marlins game, I park in someone's yard and pay cash. When my daughter got married someone's *abuela* made me beautiful favors at a fraction of what they would cost in a store. The guy who fixes my car can make it run without ordering a part from anywhere. When I went for my driver's test, a band of shadow instructors ran me through the course ahead of time, for cash. . ."

"So there's a black market in Miami," interrupted agent Hammond. "What does that have to do with this investigation?"

"It's not a black market," Shawna explained, "it's a culture, it's a community of people who know how to make things happen on their own initiative when it won't happen another way. It's like sailing 90 miles over water on a 1957 Chevy. You've had weeks of complaints from the community who feel they are under attack. If you don't take them seriously they are going to defend themselves and fight back, their way, and in a way you won't even know," Shawna scanned the room full of irritated, skeptical expressions.

"Do you have any direct knowledge of any such organized group?" asked Hammond.

"No, but," started Shawna.

"Then we are done hearing from you," Hammond stated.

Shawna quickly left the conference room, picked up her desk phone and called her kids. She was more than angry. She sensed a change in air pressure – a sure sign of a coming Hurricane. Despite the prevailing opinion of the men in the office, she was sure of one thing: she would not be around when this storm struck.

She propped the phone on her shoulder while shooting an email off to human resources about her vacation days.

Her youngest, Anthony, answered the phone. "Want to go to Disney World with mommy?" Shawna said, gathering up her things.

22

THE CONNECTION

Back in the basement at St. Mary's, Juan was meeting with the brother of the priest who started Pedro Pan.

"Let me show you something I have not shared with many over the years," said Father John. Juan followed Father John down several corridors to a large old wooden door. The priest drew a key from his robe.

"I didn't see this in Raul's journal. What is it, a crypt?" asked Juan.

"No, Juan, though some are buried here, this is not a crypt. The limestone tunnels are like a labyrinth. Some tunnels are dead ends. Some have collapsed over time with the excavation of large buildings. Raul's journal could not have documented every opening. For you and your friends to get around, you will need an expert.

I want you to meet an old friend," Father John said as the door opened. Juan took a step back, looking at something like an apparition. A flickering lantern intermittently revealed white hair atop a deeply lined face. As his eyes adjusted, he saw the outstretched hand of Chief Ahchoko.

23

THE OTTER

Deep into a limestone cavern, Chief Ahchoko walked with Juan.
Juan had to crawl through some areas, and Chief Ahchoko stopped
periodically and shared some juice from a flask as they traveled.
Dampness in the tunnels grew, and eventually they came upon a
lagoon. Tied to the rocky wall were small boats and beat-up, small
submarines. Weapon stashes were everywhere. Juan made notes
of the entrances along the Miami River.

"My grandsons figured out how to operate these submarines. If
you agree to remove them from our tunnels, and keep the diagram
of the tunnels to yourselves, we will show your people how to use
them." Juan nodded.

"Also we have an otter for you. He is held in the next cave,"
Ahchoko said as he walked carefully ahead.

Ahchoko escorted Juan to a small crevice in a nearby cave. There
sat a man in black clothes, pale and thin. He spoke Cuban Spanish.

Ahchoko poured juice from another flask into the man's throat. After several minutes, Ahchoko allowed Juan to speak to him.

"I'm a double agent. I couldn't find Raul to update him on the plans. Castro's agents murdered him. I was trying to hide down here while I figured things out. What day is it?" the otter asked.

"Friday," said Juan.

"The attack is in two days at 3:30 p.m. Castro is sending a large submarine to the middle of the river to blow up downtown. Others are planned further up the river. The mayor and other hostages are being held in a large sub under Biscayne Bay." The man's voice trailed off. He looked very weak.

Juan thanked Ahchoko. "Guide me back to the church, I have a lot of work to do."

Ahchoko motioned to two Miccosukees who had emerged from the dark. They loaded the otter onto a pallet to pull back to the reservation.

"We'll take him to our reservation until the proper authorities verify his identity," they assured Juan.

24

CUBA LIBRE

Columbus Day weekend was the perfect cover for Castro's operation. Flotillas of drunken revelers would hide the subs on their way to Miami. The Coast Guard would be focused on the action on the water – not below it.

Juan's plans were coming together. Weapons, including missiles, had been loaded onto small subs, which were ready to depart from the river. Planes were fueling up. Small fast boats were ready to go.

On Sunday, Juan went to mass in disguise. He watched his daughter and her family and then waited in the rectory. They were ushered in for a tearful reunion.

"*Te amo*," said Juan as he hugged them all.

Then he went by the domino park and enjoyed a cigar with his friends. The police were too busy to maintain surveillance on the park. At 1:30 his friends folded the table and drove to the river. There they boarded a fast boat. Juan thought he heard a cheer as their boat blasted out of the Miami River, bound for Cuba.

Biscayne Bay swelled with boatloads of partiers. Under the cover of water, the first of the exile's subs departed. Juan's boat had slowed to weave through the party boats. He felt like he was dancing drunk at a wedding: happy but starting to feel nervousness. Soon the throngs of boaters thinned and Juan and his party were speeding towards Cuba.

Suddenly, an undersea war erupted. Missiles were launched at Castro's submarine flotilla. As the first missile struck, the U.S. Military's alert system jolted alive with lights and alarms. The speed of its response, however, did not take into account just how close Cuba is to Miami.

The Coast Guard was busy enforcing safety regulations among the Columbus Day regatta boaters when the battle began. They found themselves caught in a web of party boats as emergency orders were given.

The Coast Guard command decided defense was the top priority and closed in on the Miami River, ordering all other vessels to return to port. As a Coast Guard cutter approached the river, two subs escorted by a small boat forced a large sub to the surface. The Coast Guard immediately seized and boarded the sub. After entering the sub, the guardsmen hoisted up three people. First pulled out was Berti - severely dehydrated and blinded by the sun, but ecstatic to be above water in daylight. Next was Armando Ortega, with a bruised, tear-stained face. He hugged each of his rescuers tightly. Last was the Mayor, disheveled, with broken glasses. He held up a peace sign with his hands, and fainted into the arms of a rescuer.

Meanwhile Juan and his compatriots were going full throttle to Cuba, flying U.S. and Cuban flags. Above, the buzz of small, exile-operated planes escorting the boats could be heard. Soon U.S. fighter jets drowned out the buzzing planes.

The roar of the fast boat and the fighter jets overwhelms Juan's senses. He shuts his eyes against the ocean spray and imagines Castro in a ridiculous tracksuit, belying the old dictator's pathetic need to broadcast his own delusion of fitness. Juan seems to see Castro ranting, waving a cigar in jerky circles, as news of the attack's failure begins to arrive. He hears Castro's raspy voice crackling out muffled orders – punctuated by gasps of breath. He imagines panic spreading among Castro's cronies and aides, as explosions jar them into running for cover.

Against reason, Castro cannot accept that the execution of his last wish is a fiasco.

He is still mouthing orders as he rises and gropes for his walker. The oversized tracksuit falls open as Castro becomes upright, revealing a hospital gown and medical bags. Castro looks around for help, and reaches out his right hand to grab one of the aides hurrying past him. The aide fades out of sight, and Castro's arm remains outstretched. The momentum of Castro's reach continues to carry him to the right, and in slow motion, Castro body lists as his balance shifts away from the walker.

Juan watches as, one by one, the fingers of Castro's left hand follow each other in a right-sided slide, until the last finger on his left hand loses its grip on the cold aluminum bar. The tennis balls stuck on the walker's rear feet glide silently ahead, and Castro falls.

Serenity overcomes Juan as he opens his eyes. Suddenly, the coast of Juan's homeland rises before him. He stands arm in arm with his long-time friends. Juan feels the boat is shaking and asks the driver to slow down.

"But Juan, we are almost there! Why slow now?" says the driver.

Smoke is rising from the coast. Juan is wet with sweat, salt water, and tears. As his eyes follow a plume of smoke up towards the clouds, he sees a bright light split the horizon. At that moment Juan speaks his last words:

"Cuba Libre."

EPILOGUE

Rick and Joe woke to the ground shaking. Dirt was dropping in small chunks from the ceiling of the cave. In unison they jumped up – "Let's get out of here!" they screamed.

"Dochi stood up from where she had stayed to watch them.

"Sorry guys. We couldn't risk you revealing these caves to the authorities," Dochi said. The caves rumbled, and a rock fell nearby. There weren't any weapons in sight. Dochi continued, "a battle is being fought with the guns and submarines from the tunnels. It's being fought undersea, and most of the tunnels will be destroyed," she said.

Nothing made sense, but the ground was definitely rumbling.

"What the hell is going on?" Rick yelled, looking for the best way out.

"Come quickly. I'll guide you back to your campsite," said Dochi, taking Joe's hand.

Rick and Joe followed Dochi through the black caverns and tunnels to her small boat. A fighter jet screamed overhead as Rick and Joe came into daylight. Mildly disoriented, they sat on the metal seats and Dochi started the boat back to the glades.

"The drug dealers you guys have been looking for aren't here. We take care of any such intruders. The weapons belonged to people trying to destroy our land all the way from the reservation to the bay. Thanks to my grandfather and some other old men, they won't be back – ever," Dochi looked up to the darkening sky. "You have no reason to stay here, but know you are welcome as long as you like," she said, giving Joe a long look. Rick was silent.

Joe and Rick returned to their campsite before nightfall. They immediately phoned the captain, but there was no connection. The satellite signal seemed to be blocked.

"Just as well," said Rick. "Think about it. Think about us trying to tell the Captain we had a Miccosukee guide show us around some tunnels with guns and submarines, and by the way, there are no longer guns, submarines or tunnels. Then we explain that we were knocked out and awoke to an undersea war, escaping in the nick of time. What do you think the Captain would say?

"You guys are crazy, is what he would say," replied Joe.

"Loco!" Rick laughed, as he reached for the peanut butter.

Loco

ABOUT THE AUTHOR

Karen Grossman is a resident of Miami, Florida. She is an attorney who enjoys her family, writing, and photography.

Her other titles include *Beyond Batteries: A Mother's Hurricane Survival Guide*.

www.ingramcontent.com/pod-product-compliance
Lightning Source LLC
Chambersburg PA
CBHW070348300526
45791CB00023B/1157